Okras are not Pretty
Growing up on the island of Barbados

Arlene Banfield

TABLE OF CONTENTS

Dedication
Acknowledgements

~To Ma~

Good-byes are not forever
Good-byes are not the end
They simply mean I'll miss you
Until we meet again

    She wore a smile that would warm your heart, and there was a lot of love wrapped up in her four-foot frame.

    I decided not to write a story for her because you'll find her presence in just about every snippet I've written on these pages. And, her spirit is too much for a snippet. You'll read about her quiet dignity and fair-minded judgment, and if you look closely enough, you'll pick up on the special moments we shared—just the two of us. Her love was unconditional and as the years past, I knew without being told, that I was one fortunate young lady. And so, I dedicate this volume to her memory in hopes that, even though I never said the words out loud to her, she knew that I loved her with all my heart and am grateful that she took me in and cared for me as her own for eleven long years.

    'Til we meet again!

ACKNOWLEDGMENTS

Grandchildren
Thank you for asking questions about my young days living on an island. Your inquisitive mind was the perfect incentive for me to think about this legacy of memories and love. I wanted you to know something about your Mimi [grandma] long before I became grandma.

Son and daughter
You grew up at a time when I had a predilection for talking about 'back when.' Thank you for your indulgence. My son, you were my cheering squad and collaborator. I will try to complete your mystical story.

Childhood friends
Special thanks for your help in refreshing my memory of some events.

My Chateauguay sister @ R & R Ltd.
In the production of this volume, I give you a huge hug and thank you for your skill and due diligence. I could not have done this without you. You are a treasure.

Somerset, Ink.
My writing sisters, you critiqued and encouraged. Just when I needed it, you gave me a nudge to keep writing. Just so you know, I will finish my novel.

Husband
You listened, read and let me know when something didn't sound just right. I can't wait to write *your* story.

Special note: I took poetic license not to use real names in some of these stories.

A Friendship Lost

We shared everything—gossip, personal items, food, and the best thing of all, we shared the same name: Alva...it was her first, my middle. It was the defining bond. In our identical navy uniform and white blouse, we looked so much alike, we could have passed for sisters. We were the proverbial *two peas in a pod*. Who would have thought that such a bond could ever be broken!

Alva and I were eleven years old and students at St. Silas' Girls School on the beautiful island of Barbados. The school was just a few doors down from St. Silas' Boys, our male-inhabited counterpart--something that made life at school most exciting. Our school was a reddish brown building that sat back from the road in distinguished charm. After going through the gate, there were two main entrances--the first to the far left for visiting dignitaries and the headmistress; the second for teachers and a third leading to the back of the building for students. There was a narrow gutter that ran the full length of the side of the building, curving towards the front property and down to the street where the overflow of rainwater ran off. Once we jumped the gutter, we spent many happy days in the one-room schoolhouse, writing essays, mastering arithmetic, learning about the crusades and the best time of all, having fun in arts and crafts. I can still make the crepe paper roses that we perfected in Mrs. Robinson's class and if challenged I might even remember how to weave a basket. One day a week we spent in the outdoor gardens, either planting or tending the glorious assortment of flowers up front or the succulent vegetables in the back. Our days were filled from nine o'clock in the morning to three o'clock in the afternoon, with two recesses in between.

Alva and I were, of course, in the same form. In another year we would be leaving that school. If fortunate, we would be moving on to secondary school, and like our education, our friendship would continue and flourish. As it happened, that was not to be the case.

One day, life at school was moving along as usual. Shortly after eleven o'clock in the morning, as was the custom, classes were dismissed for the first recess of the day. Each group had lined up for a snack of biscuits and milk and then dispersed to the outer areas of the schoolyard. But this day I had other things on my mind besides the crispy treats. Hoping I would not be noticed, I lagged behind and moved stealthily next to my best friend's book bag. The room was quiet; no one was in sight. I opened the bag and took several sheets of notepaper. I felt very pleased with myself, thinking I had outsmarted my friend. I closed the notebook, and just as I was about to put the bounty into my own bag, I felt a hand on my shoulder. Shaking with fear, I looked up into the chastising eyes of Mrs. Bishop, the meanest teacher in the school. "Come," she said.

Following meekly, paper in hand, I arrived at the office of the Head Mistress, Mrs. Small. She was a rather large woman who suffered with a bad leg, the result of a break in her ankle. She walked with a cane. Mrs. Small ruled the school with an iron will and a leather strap. A visit to her office, which was actually a desk on a raised platform, left no question as to the outcome. Corporal punishment was law. I knew I would be punished, and quickly decided I'd have to talk fast to explain my actions. If I were lucky, I thought, I might escape with two or three lashes. That was the norm for giving the wrong answers to test questions, arriving late to school, or any other form of transgression.

I told my story with passionate meekness. One week earlier, Alva had asked if I would lend her some notepaper. She promised to give some back soon as she was able to purchase her own. I didn't hesitate for a moment; after all, she was my best friend. I would do anything to make her happy. But now, here it was, a full day after she had bought a new supply of paper. I had asked her to keep her promise. She refused. I was hurt and angry. I had given her half of my already meager supply and I was now down to my last few sheets. I walked away feeling very unhappy that my friend could be so unkind.

"You know the rules at St. Silas," Mrs. Small pronounced. "You do not take what is not yours," she reminded me.

I nodded, tears running down my face. I would not be getting off easy. As far as Mrs. Small was concerned I was caught stealing. I prepared for my lashes right there and then, but I was caught in another surprise. The headmistress instructed Mrs. Bishop to cut recess and bring all the students back into the schoolhouse. I was left standing, awaiting my fate.

Meanwhile, in a chair now centered in the front of the open room, Mrs. Small sat, waiting---with her leather strap. Soon all the students were back, each sitting erect in her seat, not knowing what to expect from the interrupted recess. I can only surmise Mrs. Small savoring the moment, for I dared not move my eyes from the floor. There was not a murmur as she told the students what I had done. Her final words to the rapt audience were, "Let what I am about to do serve as a lesson to each of you." With that she instructed me to lie across her lap. She then gave me the whipping of my life.

After several lashes that stung my legs and thighs, I stopped crying. I became outraged that I should be punished for taking what I considered rightfully mine, and for being humiliated before all my schoolmates. It was too much. With every sting of the strap, I plotted revenge. The tears stopped.

If I had anything to say about it, my now ex-friend would never again borrow from anyone; furthermore, I'd be waiting for her after school. Revenge on the headmistress would take a bit of planning. I was so busy plotting and my anger so deep, I didn't realize the lashes had stopped until Mrs. Small said, "You may take your seat."

I rose with as much dignity as I could gather, doing my best to keep the tears from resurfacing. I crept back to my seat next to Alva, who was now too scared to even look at me: she too had broken a golden rule that day, the rule of friendship. I didn't dwell on her, however. Her fate was already determined. I was focused on Mrs. Small and it was then that I remembered her bad leg.

Mrs. Small's injury had caused her leg to be permanently deformed. She always needed help ascending and descending the back steps to the schoolyard, and I promised myself, I would be waiting to help her. Some of my classmates were quick to aid and abet in my plans for revenge; I would be getting justice for all punishments ever handed down. "Man, I wudda tek a bite outta she fat leg while she had me spread cross she lap like dat," offered my friend, Myrna, who would have preferred immediate comeuppance. Maybe she would have too; she was the most brave and vocal of our circle of friends.

Of course, my opportunities for revenge never came. Alva carefully avoided me outside of the classroom until I grew tired of the cat and mouse, and either word leaked or the eager look I wore each time Mrs. Small came near the steps made my intentions crystal clear. During my remaining days at the school, she never again asked me for assistance navigating the back steps.

My friendship with Alva suffered an irreparable break. My days at school had lost some of the joy I once took for granted. I missed the moments of secret talk about Andrew and Michael, the "boyfriends" we claimed without their knowledge. Now when I wanted to take a surreptitious peek beyond the gates of the boys' school, I no longer had my friend to share the fun or the chance of getting caught. I suffered a glut of emotions and a broken heart. When I left the island a year later, it was without reconciliation with my once good friend.

By the Moonlight

A night with a full moon on the tiny island of Barbados is the stuff the calypso balladeers sing about. It is a night that charms lovers into walking hand in hand on the soft sands of the Caribbean ocean. But often these are also nights that young children get to stay outside just a little bit longer to play their made-up games or the old familiar ones.

It was on such a night that my cousin, Esmee and I and a few of our local friends gathered to play an old favorite, hide and seek. The moon-filled sky lit up every corner of our small world outside our chattel house: through the trees, and up the hill through the craggy rocks and spiky grass, it was as though the day would never end.

We were not afraid to be out on nights likes these; at least not about unknown creatures waiting to snatch us up. Our fear came from the thought of getting tagged and having to be the one to find the allusive "it." Our games were usually non-eventful, and we'd end the night exhausted, and eager for another moonlight night. That is, until one night when things took an awful turn.

We assembled under our favorite tree, *"Home."* It was a spindly thing with branches hanging so low we could just reach up and touch the leaves. On rainy days, a favorite pastime was standing next to that tree and shake rain water down on any unsuspecting soul who made the mistake of walking under it at the wrong moment.

I was first to be "it" and quickly tagged the next victim. Esmee was good at the game and rarely got tagged. When it was finally her turn to be *it*, I wasted no time while she counted. I took off up the hill just yards from the house. Zigzagging through the rocks I settled behind a large boulder. In no time I heard Estelle getting close. I jumped up and took off back down the hill to reach the safety of the tree.

Halfway down I slipped on some gravel and went, elbows first, sliding into a prickly shrub. I wailed in pain as I got back up and stood on wobbling feet. I grabbed my right elbow which felt as though it had separated from my arm and gingerly worked my way down the hill. When I stopped at the tree I noticed blood all over my hands and clothes. Everyone soon gathered and we all stared in shock at the blood, the ragged flesh and exposed bones.

Only life or death meant a trip to a doctor or hospital which was miles away. Adding to that, it was late at night and we had no transportation. We walked everywhere. Ma, my substitute mother did what most folks did in these instances. She cleaned up the cut, removing bits of gravel. As my tears flowed, she took the leaf of freshly cut aloes, peeled, sliced, heated it and then applied it to my elbow, then wrapped the area as tight as I could bear it so that the bones would knit. Aloes (called Aloe Vera elsewhere) grew wild all over the island and was the homemade remedy for headaches, bellyaches, cuts and bruises. It was even mixed with molasses and grain and fed to the animals as a preventative against disease. I was only slightly comforted that I didn't have to eat the bitter plant.

It took several weeks for my elbow to heal and I was left with an ugly scar and a permanently deformed elbow bone. Even so, I carry it proudly as my "identifying mark" on my US citizenship papers.

Every now and then the spot itches, giving me a gentle reminder of that carefree time. The memory is sweet. It is of moonlight and laughter and secret places.

Collecting Firewood

One of the most unique things about our home was the kitchen. It was not attached to the house, it stood maybe six feet away, almost a little house by itself. It had storage for food, a table used mostly as a temporary resting place for hot foods and a bench for waiting: waiting for food to cook or the most exciting thing of all, waiting for baked breads from the large brick oven. Next to the oven was the huge fireplace that could hold two large pots at a time. And because it was so huge, the fireplace required lots of wood on a regular basis. The one chore we didn't mind was going on the wood gathering hunt once a week. From our house we took a well-worn path, lined on one side by papaya and lime trees, pumpkin vines and green pea bushes, and on the other by sugar cane. The end of the path led to the edge of our land and the most idyllic place I knew.

Usually our trek was to collect dried branches from the bamboo forest and bushes a few yards off. The bamboo forest was actually a small patch of land densely populated with the majestic trees. Though naturally wild, these grew as if someone had blueprinted the spot. The aging process of the trees provided the dry shoots we used to light the large fire in the kitchen in which our meals were prepared. When not trekking for cinder wood, we took the path just to go to our special place on the hill. There we would sit under a tall pine tree, with the breeze blowing in our faces. Sometimes the breeze was more of a gutsy wind that made us catch our breath. From this spot we could see the lush green countryside in the distance. On occasion we could see the smoke rising up from the chimneys at the plantations and sugarcane factories in St. Andrews, another parish, miles away. Below us was the gully, dense with an assortment of trees bearing fruits with names like gooseberries, dounce, ackees, and tamarinds. Some bore nuts called macaws. Magnificent ferns in light and dark green shades filled the floor of the gully. There were stately flowers like the flamboyant, hibiscus, magnolias and lilies, and wild ones with names I can't recall, growing on vines, bushes, trees. Their aroma filled the air.

A day of fun meant taking the jagged path down from the hilltop through the gully to pick and eat our fill of fruit and gather some of the flowers that came in more colors than a dozen rainbow. One favorite was a bulbous-type, that when massaged, the rubbery portion of the flower became so pliant it could be blown up into a tiny balloon. We'd then pop it and squeal in delight. We couldn't resist the ferns with their white powdery underside that tickled our feet as we passed. We would break off a few stems and stamp our arms and legs with the powdered side, creating beautiful lacy white designs on our dark skins. We did all this while being careful to avoid disturbing the beehives that were nestled in some of the trees. On separate occasions, my older cousin, Ken, who was fourteen, would condescendingly join us so that he could show his prowess by extracting a honeycomb without disturbing the bees. We liked when he showed off because it meant we'd get to taste the honey. But more often, feeling full from the fruit and delighted with our temporary fern tattoos, we'd climb back up the hill to rest on the grass under our favorite pine tree.

We didn't talk much. We sat and watched the humming birds as they flew from flower to flower; or we listened to the cooing doves as they came as close to us as they thought safe. We always tried to catch one: there was fun in the chase. A special treat was the antics and yapping of a monkey or two jumping from limb to limb as though playing hide and seek with us. And finally we might collect some of the pine nuts that fell from the tree to use in our games, or after wrapping them in silver paper, they would decorate our tree during the Christmas holiday. With all the diversions at hand, the job of collecting wood was just the excuse we needed to escape for a few hours.

This, That and De Third

Mention being born on a Caribbean island and an image of sunny skies, blue waters and days lolling on pink sand almost immediately comes to mind. No doubt there are those who do enjoy this life pictured on tempting postcards. The reality for most of us is a day of routine jobs and responsibilities designed to make life comfortable. As a small child, I had my list of things to do to contribute to that comfort and bring food to the table. I never thought much about the pink sand and blue waters and didn't mind most of the things I had to do; not that it would have mattered.

There were a few I actually liked. One was taking the sheep out to pasture and turning them loose to graze. This was my opportunity to sit and daydream about going to America...and boy could I dream. I conjured up pictures in my head that were so real, when I finally landed in America, I kept looking for the big gray house surrounded by tall trees with drooping branches. It was a staple in my daily dreams.

Gathering fresh greens for the rabbits was also not a bad deal. It was another chance to play and it was fun searching out just the right grasses, being careful to avoid anything dangerous to the little furry cottontails. I enjoyed watching the rabbits munching away on what obviously was a delicious treat to them. Beautiful flowers, many attracting colorful butterflies blended with the greens to distract me from the mundane.

I was not so easily distracted from the tedious job of sprinkling clothes. That activity followed washday, when Ma would scrub the clothes on the washboard. Once the clothes were soaked in the "blue" mixture used to help whiten, and then rinsed, Ma would lay the clothes flat on the grass in an area set aside just for that purpose. It was far away from where the domestic animals and fowls could do damage. Of course, we had no control over the wild birds flying overhead but I don't recall ever seeing evidence of their flight. My job was to keep the clothes moist every hour or so by sprinkling them with fresh water for a day. I never understood the dynamics of this ritual, but it obviously worked. We always had the whitest whites imaginable.

My least favorite thing to do was gathering eggs from under the house where the chickens roosted. On hands and knees, I crawled to reach the nest, being careful not to land in the chicken poop. Most of the time I was successful, but every now and again, I would plop right down in it and get that mess all over my clothes. But even in that dirty task, there was a pleasant side—Ma usually made me two eggs for breakfast instead of the one everyone else was served. It was our little secret.

There were no unpleasant effects in churning butter, that is, if I didn't think on the many hours it took to turn the milk, fresh from the cow, into creamy butter. Thankfully I didn't have to perform the first stage of the butter-making process: milking the cow. I suppose I was really too puny for that. From the huge pails, Ma, or most likely Da, would apportion the milk in bottles--about half full. We children each got one bottle and took our position on a seat that we'd make as comfortable as possible. It was going to be a long sit down.

Not surprisingly, I found time during those long hours of churning to dream of what awaited me when I finally got to America.

With the bottle resting on one leg, I would grasp the bottle by the neck and rock it back and forth for hours. The length of time depended on how fast and steady I rocked. The end result was not the Land O' Lakes kind of butter, instead it was a thick creamy substance that was then set aside to solidify. This exhausting task came with a treat: hot buttered freshly brick-oven baked bread. And just how did these two things come together so perfectly timed? Ma and Da, working in unison to make life sweet.

There was nothing especially sweet about re-stuffing our mattress; but perhaps it was twice a year, I can't remember now, Ma would let us know it was time to go to the cane field. There may be a few raised eyebrows asking the question, what does sugar cane have to do with a mattress. Ah, it's so simple. Not only did we depend on cane for sugar and syrup, we made good use of those beautiful shoots from the top of the stalk. Soft and feathery like the plumes of a proud peacock, the shoots, which we called cane arrow, were broken into small pieces. We filled the open sack that was the form for the mattress until it was bulging. Our first night on the newly stuffed mattress was cause for many sticks and pricks, because no matter how feathery, there were still bits of hard stalk that found their way into the mix. It took several nights, while we yearned for the familiarity of our old mattress, for things to eventually settled. Soon enough we'd be back snuggling on our spot in the crowded bed. Who would have known there was a Sealy in my future!

I won't say that those were 'the good old days,' because there's no question, I favor modern conveniences. I will declare that looking back on those days does exactly what it is supposed to do; it fills me with joy.

Simple Simon met a pieman
Going to the fair
Says Simple Simon to the pieman
Let me taste your ware

Says the pieman to Simple Simon
Show me first your penny
Says Simple Simon to the pieman
Indeed I have not any

De Lorry Mash Up

Sheryl was one of the girls that everyone envied. She was tall and elegant with a smile that lit up the room. Sheryl lived in Orange Hill, so close to the school, she didn't have to walk the four miles my cousin and I walked—but neither was she lucky enough to have the experience of pilfering mangoes from Waterhall Plantation or taking the shortcut through Apes Hill to over-indulge on tamarinds growing wild in the orchard. I guess you could say Sheryl was one of the rich kids in our circle. Her family had a store and a big house that sat up on a hill. They owned one of the few phonographs on the island, and often we would hear sweet classical music flowing out to us as we walked to and from school. But these things were just matter-of-fact for Sheryl; she never acted "poor-great" like some others who had a little more than the rest of us.

Sheryl was one of the true friends I hated to say good-bye to when I left the island. And it was years after that I finally saw her again. We've had a good time reminiscing about our school days at Saint Silas, and life in general. We talked about dallying with the boys at St. Silas Boys' School, catching a rare smile or hello when no adults were within scolding distance. So, when I told her about my plans to write these essays, she eagerly reminded me of an incident I had forgotten.

One morning, my friends who lived in Springhead, the village next to mine, brought the news to me that Sheryl's grandfather's lorry had turned over in the gully with a load of sugar canes. Her grandfather and two workers were making their way to the factory where the freshly harvested cane would be processed into sugar and syrup. My friends were some of the first on the scene: a gully just a short distance from my home. They stopped to get me and we were off to school, passing the word of the accident to everyone we met along the way. We were human telephones in the absence of the electrical machines.

Anytime there was an accident in or near a gully, everyone expected the worse. These deep ravines, along the side of the road were a traveler's nightmare whether on foot, horse and cart or by automobile. People on foot sped past the darkness out of fear of the imagined creatures that dwelled within. It took expert handling for a driver to maneuver the narrow roads without flipping over into the gully: there was no such thing as a guardrail.

There was a well-known and notoriously dangerous gully on the road that we traveled to reach Bridgetown, the island capital. Lancaster Gully, a bottomless abyss, had claimed the lives of several people some years earlier, when a truck went over the side. That accident lived in the minds and hearts of every Bajan; even those of us, who learned of it by listening to the grown folks talk. Each time we had to pass this gully by bus, I held my breath 'till I could no longer see the black hole.

The gully in Sheryl's accident was not nearly as deep and frightening as Lancaster, but it was almost as scary. So when news of the accident finally reached the Endeavor, it was a relief for Sheryl's family to hear that "no one was hurt, but de lorry mash up."

Under the Flambo Tree

Life in The Spring, Saint James was close to idyllic, but this maybe a view from my grownup nostalgia. One thing is true, I spent much of my time daydreaming about coming to America. But when I wasn't daydreaming, I enjoyed lots of fun times with my two cousins.

One of my favorite things to do was to go to the orchard. Actually, it wasn't really an orchard, just a wild patch of trees, plants and flowers that we children named the orchard. It was our get-a-way place when chores were done and the grownups were too occupied with other matters to find something to occupy us. There was tamarind, golden apple, plum and lime trees, growing wild and plentiful.

The trip there accomplished many things: we had our fill of the ripe fruit, and afterwards it was a chance to walk through the patch of ferns nestled under the huge flamboyant tree, commonly called flambo. We spent hours playing; stamping our arms and legs with the white powder that grew under the belly of the intricately serrated leaves. My cousins and I tried to outdo each other in making the prettiest, most elaborate designs. I always took my time in everything I did, and this was no different. I was never in a rush to finish. I enjoyed the fun and challenge of making the designs that brought me some measure of contentment. Not much could top these things, except perhaps the view from hill.

Just a few yards from the orchard, there stood a huge windmill at the crest of a hill, overlooking the most spectacular view of the Scotland district. We called it Scotland Yard—not really knowing why. My guess is we named it after the yard of fame in our mother country, England. Scotland district seemed close enough to walk to, but that was just an illusion. The exciting thing about standing at the windmill was the breathtaking wind that blew up from the lea below. At times it seemed that if we didn't find a nearby branch to hold on to, that swirling wind would take us right across the grass and drop us into the nearby ponds.

We stayed at the windmill until we could no longer stand the constant intake of breath necessary to enjoy the view. We finally left, feeling as good and cool as having a refreshing sea bath.

Flambo trees are on almost every corner on the island but of course, more bountiful in the country. I was born miles away from my favorite flambo tree, in a small town called Rock Dundo. It was between the towns of Upper Carlton and Lower Carlton. I didn't live there very long. At the age of two, I was taken to the Spring and left in the care of Ma and Crongie. The Spring was as close to Rock Dundo as night is to day. In rock Dundo we could shop at the local rum shops and dry goods store. The bus to Bridgetown went right through the main street, but in the Spring, when we needed groceries, we had to walk several miles to a place called Rock Hall in the next parish.

To get to Rock Hall, we had to pass through Springhead. Of course, we children always found ways to dawdle or get into some mischief along the way. We always found time to pick golden apples on the Kings' property. This was never a real problem, since they didn't mind. But just past the Kings was the Springhead plantation. There was no way to pass the plantation without arousing the large dogs (two of them) that guarded the front entrance. Thankfully there was a long walkway from the street to the entrance, so we had a small measure of safety from the animals. As soon as they sensed our presence, they could come barreling and barking down the walkway at breakneck speed. Just when we thought we were dog meat, they would come to a screeching halt as though they were on a leash or equipped with some other restraining device. They would then turn around and head back to the front door. This happened each time, but we were always cautious, carrying a long stick, just in case they came past that invisible dividing line.

Once we passed the plantation, it was time to play again. We had to walk over a little bridge that took us over a good size pond.

There were wild ducks in the pond and it seemed like good fun to toss small stones at them. Thankfully our aim was worse than our intensions. I don't recall ever hitting any of them.

After passing the pond, there wasn't much left to distract us from our appointed destination. We'd arrive at the shop and gather all the items Ma sent us to get. These were usually flour, sugar, vanilla, dry cod fish, and canned corn beef: all things that we couldn't grow at home.

I would much rather collect firewood, because that gave me the unrestrained pleasure of escaping to the hill and savoring my moments under the flambo tree.

London's burning, London's burning.
Fetch the engines, fetch the engines.
Fire fire, fire fire!
Pour on water, pour on water.
London's burning, London's burning

Five O'clock Whistle

The whistle at Waterhall plantation hooted away while three pair of legs ran pell-mell toward home. Late again!

Reaching home after the five o'clock whistle was sure to earn me a stern scolding from Ma if she was in a forgiving mood; otherwise it was the sting of a few lashes. But I for one often pushed my luck by getting there just ahead or at the last hoot. The reason for being late meant I was dallying with my friends and having too much fun; not worrying about the possibility of a lashing. Why would I think about clocks and whistles when there was so much mischief to sample? We had a favorite spot for said mischief.

The plantation was a reminder of slave days for the older folks, but for us it was an odd place of mystery and fun. Waterhall was a bonanza with its windmill—a real windmill, not the stuff of Don Quixote; grass stacks and a magnificent orchard. We admired the windmill from a distance and yearned to jump in the haystacks. But lush mangoes growing in the orchard were too tempting to simply admire from a distance. It was at their most lush when the loaded bunches of mangoes seemed to beckon and we youngsters just couldn't resist the temptation. We always went for the fruit.

I had to have one more escapade before leaving the island...something to reminisce over in my old age. Looking at me now no one might believe I was so daring back then. Oh, but I was.

One look at the bounty growing in the orchard and I was hooked into crawling under the barbed wire. At twelve I was pretty wiry myself and it was easy for me to maneuver my way through an opening in the fence made possible by two partners in crime doing their part by holding up a portion of the wire. Not only did I have to worry about scratching my skin, more important, I had to guard against tearing my school uniform. There would be no escaping the lash if that happened.

The navy jumper and white blouse stood out like a sign with my name on it. It was a chore to keep it clean and damage free, yet somehow, I managed. But on this day, I had to have my last hurrah—in a few weeks I'd be far away from Saint Silas Girls School and uniforms—it was worth the risk.

Why is it that "one last time" always has a ring of danger? Everything was going great—so we thought. We had checked our surroundings and there was not a watchman in sight. The quiet should have been a warning. My friends carefully pulled up their end of the barbed wire and I stuck one foot on plantation soil. No sooner had I planted my second foot did I hear, "Hold up!"

The one thing I didn't want to do was *hold up*. Faster than I thought possible, I untangled myself from the wire fence, and in one fluid motion, grabbed up my school books and took off up the cart road as if my life depended on it. It did. I just prayed that my friends were in close proximity to my escaping form.

Was it the act of pilfering forbidden fruit that made these escapades exciting, or, was it the pleasure of sinking my teeth into the soft sweet mango with its juice dripping off my chin, or could it possibly be the adrenaline that pumped at the possibility of getting caught. When I was twelve years old it was all that and more.

Gotcha

Crongie was a man of few words. When he chose to give voice to what was going on in his head, there was never a doubt as to his meaning. With just one word, he once made his meaning painfully clear to me. All he said was, "Gotcha!"

Crongie was my great uncle, but he and his wife became my caretakers when my mother left the island for America. I was only two years old at the time, but as soon as I could talk, I fell into calling him Da, just as his children did. He wife was Ma. His real name was Fitzgerald Maynard, but some adults called him Crongie when he was out of ear shot. A few tried to call him Fitz, but he only answered to Mr. Maynard. I still don't know where the name Crongie originated. I only know that in Barbados, nicknames were common and that was his. These names weren't always kind, and they usually stuck.

Da never smiled, but he didn't carry a sour expression either. His face always seemed to say he was keeping secrets.

A man of many talents, Crongie commanded respect for his strength and knowledge. He was as comfortable working the huge outdoor brick oven used for making homemade breads and cakes, as he was in the cane field. During crop time, when the sugar cane was being harvested, he was one of the lead men cutting the cane. With his strong right arm aimed high, sweat glistening off his black leathery skin, he moved along the rows like a well programmed robot. He stopped only long enough for lunch, which was usually eaten right there in the field, and then again at the five o'clock whistle when all work ended for the day.

Somehow before and after work in the field, he had time to oversee life at home. He made sure that the assortment of livestock he maintained were well tended: pigs, sheep, rabbits, chickens, guinea pigs, cows and ducks were in abundance. These were the source of our food, and he was adept at doing what was necessary to bring that food to table, whether it was slaughtering a pig or butchering a cow.

With his gruff exterior and serious demeanor, no one would ever think to find Da in the kitchen. But when it came to baking, that's exactly where you'd find him. Baking was a family activity. My cousin Esmee or I would have gone to the market for dry coconuts, flour, sugar and spices. Ma did the mixing of the ingredients after one of us sat and grated the coconut into fine flakes. When all the ingredients were well mixed, Ma rolled them into loaves and placed them lovingly into the greased pans. After that Da took over. With an oar-like spatula, some four feet in length, he gently eased the pans into the deep abyss that was the oven, cut into one wall of the outdoor kitchen. This room was almost a miniature house in its construction. Built into the side of a huge boulder, and separated by several feet from the living quarters, it held the cooking pit and an area for storing wood, a table and large tub for cleaning pots and dishes, and storage for these items. Dominating the space was the oven that extended the full depth of the outer wall which was about four feet wide by six feet deep. Because of its intimidating size and the intense heat emanating from the oven, Da was the only one to go near those spatulas or the oven. But a slice of warm coconut bread, plain pound cake, and occasionally a special delicacy of stew conkies, was worth the work, the wait, and Da's dominion in this area of our life

My cousins and I were not immune to doing foolish things—and that's where the "gotcha" came in. We knew before we started our games that messing with Da's property was a no-no. Yet, one day when we wanted to jump rope, we couldn't resist the neatly rolled rope, hanging high on a nail. It was the piece of rope that Da used to corral the cows. It may not have been too bad a crime, except that this piece was brand spanking new. We had a great time that afternoon and thought no one would be the wiser if we put the rope back exactly where we found it. We were woefully wrong.

He wasn't home long before we heard him fussing about the rope. He didn't ask any questions; he knew what was what. Before you could say *cheese on bread*, he snatched Esmee up by the scruff and gave her a lashing with his well-worn belt. I would have been next, except, wiry as always, I slipped out of his reach and took off through the canes to hide out. I had no clue how long I thought I'd get away with this ploy. The one thing I knew for sure was that Da would never wake me up to give lashes; he wasn't about being cruel. He would catch me in his own time.

It had been weeks since the incident and I must admit I had put it out of my mind and thought Da had too. One afternoon after he'd come in from work, he went about his usual chores paying no attention to me, or so I thought. I was standing next to Ma engrossed in something she was making for dinner…when out of the blue I was snatched from behind with that one-word sentence: "Gotcha." Well, he got me all right. A few lashes across my rump with that same worn belt and the score with the old cow rope was even. I screamed and fussed, more out of surprise than anything. But I had to play it out. I threatened to write and tell my mother that he had whipped me because I knew that's the last thing a caretaker wants to hear. Da looked at me like I'd lost my mind. My ranting made little impression on him; and as you might guess, I never did write any letter. Once the sting of the lashes wore off, the memory of the incident receded, but the lesson of obedience remained.

That was the first and last time I received a lashing from Da. As I said, he was a man of few words and it was not necessary for him to ever remind me to obey his rules again.

For other than that whipping, Da stands out in my mind, partly because he was such an enigma. He was stern and precise and bordered domineering. I don't ever remember him setting foot in a church, yet he could quote the bible as though he wrote it. One of his favorite pastimes was reading to us children. And as aloof as he was, we looked forward to those times. Mostly this time occurred on a rainy day when we were confined to the indoors. And what made it more special was where we gathered to listen. The Front room was usually off limits to us except on special occasions. It was reserved for entertaining special guests. This room was always pristine in its neatness. White lace curtains at the windows and dollies on each surface created a soft airy feminine touch against the dark sturdy mahogany furniture and

Da's dark stocky frame. In this setting was the family bible. It never left this room.

Perhaps it was lack of quiet and reverence in the back room that brought us to the Front room on those rainy days when we sat around Da as he read from some of his favorite bible passages: Psalm Twenty-three. He also told us about the shortest verse in the bible, "Jesus Wept," and he spoke authoritatively on the many miracles of Jesus. My limited knowledge of the bible may be thanks to Da, not the several churches I've attended in my lifetime.

Da loved snuff. And I often watched in fascination as he sat on a tree stump methodically going through the ritual of pinching and stoking snuff from a brown bag. After a while he would begin sneezing, seemingly non-stop. Why anyone would endure this torture I couldn't understand. But he seemed to enjoy himself, and it made him just a bit gentler than at other times. "It was medicinal," someone told me years later. My response, "Sure it was!"

"I didn't know you left." That was Da's greeting fourteen years later when I returned to Barbados for the first time with husband and son in tow. I tried to revisit my young days with some quick stories of certain incidents. I then spoke of life in America in hope that Da would appreciate the young woman I had grown into. I thanked him for what he'd done for me as a child. But again, the verbal exchange was mostly one sided. He hadn't changed much; he was still stingy with words and smiles. Perhaps I should have mentioned the cow rope.

Hurricanes and Avocados*

The sky slowly darkened; an eerie silence prevailed. Trees swayed and soon fruits fell from their lofty perch. Leaves flew through the air as if released from an archer's bow. Rooftops were ripped off with frightening ease. As if on cue, the clouds opened up, and a torrent of rain came crashing down.

Hurricane Janet sliced through Barbados like a warm knife in butter. We were young and foolish and getting hurt was the farthest thing from our minds. At the onset of the storm, my cousins and I did what we usually did when we heard the wind rustling through the treetops. We ran under the avocado tree that stood majestically on our property just a few yards from the front door. Its branches hung low, although not so low that we could reach the fruit, and we never were able to climb the bulging trunk no matter what ingenious ways we invented.

The avocado tree had not yet begun to yield the bounty we wanted, so we continued our play on the nearby hilltop, even as the last of the sparkling blue clouds changed to somber gray. The sting of a missile-like leaf against my cheek did not deter me from chasing my cousins through the grass and shrubs nestled between the rocks.

After a while we turned out attention back to the original object of our attention. To our delight there was now a bonanza of fallen avocados on the ground. We began to scoop them up, thrilled that we could enjoy the delicious treat without fear of punishment for knocking them down with stones. We were oblivious to the danger around us and continued our treasure hunt until a voice from inside the house warned us with one word "Come." Anyone who says Bajans talk a lot has never been disciplined by one.

It may have been five minutes later, when we heard a loud slow creaking sound. Looking out the window we saw one of the largest branches of the avocado tree break free of its sturdy limb and crash to the ground. A single word escaped from Ma as she viewed the damage... "Wuhloss!" Loosely translated, it means oh, my goodness! Or some might say, Lord have mercy. Only she understood the narrow escape we children had experienced.

Hours later we emerged from our chattel house; a little amazed that its foundation of uneven and oddly placed stones had not shifted even a little. We had survived yet another hurricane. Again, there was quiet, made more unnerving after the torrential rain and thunderous noises of the storm. It was a silence heightened by the absence of things familiar: doves did not coo, chickens had retreated to their respective roosts under the house and not a grunt was heard from the pigsty. The rabbits were cuddled in furry balls in the cages while the billy goats and sheep rested on their bellies in their pens. Thankfully we knew this phenomenon would not last long.

When it seemed safe and obvious dangers had passed, Da went about surveying the property. We children were a respectful distance behind him, keeping our sights on the other fallen fruit we'd enjoy later: plums, grapefruits, sugar apples, and soursops. We watched as Da took note of the more important aspects of our every-day life. Standing securely in its usual place at the side of the house, the water drum was overflowing so that we'd have enough water for washing for days to come. We would sleep well knowing that no windows were missing and only a few shingles were loose. Our village was one of the few that never had electricity, so there was no concern about going without light. Our trusty lanterns would be burning as usual. Our only casualty was the missing outhouse. A man of few words, we never knew until days later that Da had been sitting on the toilet when the frame was blown away by a whirling gust of wind. In our exuberant antics around the avocado tree and on the hilltop, we had missed what must have been one hilarious sight.

Days past and the adults continued to talk about the "worse hurricane" ever to hit our tiny island. We children huddled in our favorite spot to savor the lingering thrill of foraging for fruits and the feel of the wind blowing us about the hillside.

*For clarity I use the word avocado, but we islanders called this fruit a pear.

Losing Andrew

In our carefree world of pink hibiscus, humming birds, cooing doves, and days made perfect with childhood games, the last thing we thought about was death. That someone our own age would die was absolutely outside the realm of possibilities. But one day all the students at both schools, St. Silas Boys and St. Silas Girls, had to face the reality of death among us. We had lost one of our own. Shock reverberated throughout the tidy rows of each classroom and the entire district. We were numbed by the occurrence.

No one told us what took Andrew from us at such a young age; the mantra of children being seen and not heard did not change for such an affecting event. But, in fairness, perhaps the grownups didn't know either, since it happened so fast. I just know that at ten years old, he was too young, too beautiful to die.

In customary fashion, his body would be laid out in his house for a day. Burial would be later that afternoon. I had grown up being afraid of the dead but I had to see him. I wanted some answers. What was death like? Would he look the same? I just could not believe that he would never again walk the narrow street from his home to school; that there'd be no more flirting with all the girls who eyed his beautiful face. I was the leader of that pack.

Most days we admirers could be found across the street from the boy's school at the perfectly placed sweet shop. Not only did we get our never ending supply of sugar cakes, ju-C's and other tasty snacks, it gave us that rare unguarded chance to see Andrew—maybe even get a shy hello. Most of the time, my visit to the shop was simply for that *chance*, since I rarely had any money. I had dawdling down to a science, which was a feat all by itself. We children were so openly supervised by any and all adults in close proximity; it was a miracle those moments ever happened.

The only way I could see Andrew was at lunch time. I rushed ahead of my school chums and headed of Mrs. Gilkes' lunch counter. But instead of going there I crossed the street and walked up to the door of Andrew's house. I tapped softly – the occasion seemed to call for it. An adult came to the door. Unlike any other time when I'd be questioned to the very depth of my being, this day I was ushered in. I was grateful for anything that didn't steal my courage. I was told, "Come," and I followed the woman through the open curtains separating the laying out room from the front room. There were others in the room, but I hardly noticed as my eyes focused on the body stretched out on the divan. He was wearing his familiar Sunday suit. His hands were folded across his chest and when I finally gathered the nerve to look at his face, I was stunned. Cotton wool was stuffed in his nose and mouth. Each eye was covered with a penny. Where was my beautiful Andrew? I backed out of the room and ran all the way back to school. I never told anyone that I went. I was too upset.

The days following the funeral were long and dreary. Missing from the school yard was the jovial noise of morning breaks and lunchtime games. Mother Nature seemed to join in our melancholy because it was exceptionally rainy for several days; even the sun had lost its smile.

Okras are not Pretty

Whip up a pot of cou-cou topped with fricasseed salt fish and you have a treat for the gods...the Bajan gods, that is. Today you can count me among the many that enjoy this meal. But there was a time when even a king's ransom couldn't get me to eat this island delicacy. When I was a little girl growing up in the Spring, a tiny village in the island of Barbados, my family, like most, enjoyed this meal at least twice a month. That was when I adopted my sour face, although I didn't need to. Each time Ma made it, she always cooked something else for me. But not liking the taste didn't stop me from appreciating the work that went into preparing the dish.

It began with picking the ripest okras. But the first thing I had to do was get to them. This involved walking through the sugar cane field. From the house, I took the worn path between the pig pen and the rabbit coop, past the overhanging orange tree. Separating the head high sugar cane, I stomped my way to the okra bush growing near the edge of our property. The rough leaves of the okra bush scratched my skin as I dug down and through the dense foliage to find the ripe, ugly fruit, masquerading as a vegetable.

After I gathered enough of the fruit with its odd shape and deep green color, I snipped the hard end closest to the stalk. When I returned to the house, I dropped them in a big bowl to wash. That's where my part of making cou-cou ended. After rinsing off what mother-nature left on the okras, Ma dropped the bounty in a pot of boiling water. She never cut them up in fancy slices or cubes—they went into the pot whole. I cringe to discuss what they looked like once they were cooked: soft slimy goo mixed with tiny gray bead-like seeds—the whole thing now a blackish green.

Setting this mixture aside, Ma started the next step in making the cou-cou. It was magical to watch the lumps of dry cornmeal turn into a smooth, yellow mush. She then slowly added some of the okra and the liquid to the mix. It took a strong arm and a good cou-cou stick to *'turn cornmeal'* and the stick was not used for any other purpose. Flat and smooth, the wooden stick was shaped like a cricket bat. It's the shape that made it easier to 'turn' ('mix') the cornmeal.

After the cornmeal mixture was set, it was usually served in a bowl surrounded with a toping of remaining okra and a heaping serving of sauce made of shredded salted fried codfish. Getting the codfish just right was another feat. Now, it had to be salted, but too much salt and the effort would be like frying ice [wasted time]. So, the first thing done was to soak that fish either overnight or for several hours. Toss that water, rinse and break the fish into tiny bite size pieces. The fish was then simmered in a combination of tomatoes, onions and an assortment of fresh herbs. Chief among these were marjoram and thyme. And *'if you're looking for trouble,'* add some good old fashion hot sauce made with special home grown hot peppers.

Cou-cou and salt fish was considered a poor man's meal, perhaps because after that meal, you could go a day before you got hungry again. I was not much impressed with all that. I simply could not take the grittiness of the meal under my tongue, or the slime and look of the okras. So, it came as no surprise when Ma finished making this stomach-filling dish, she would make something special for me: my favorite was rice and pigeon peas with pigtails.

I wonder what Ma would say today if she could see me devouring a bowl of that age old dish and making a dash for seconds. I don't even mind the okras–but ugh, they're still ugly.

Pomp and Circumstance

It was a clear, beautiful day in February of 1955.   There was no hint of the periodic showers as natural to the coral isle of Barbados as its crystal blue waters. At Saint Silas Girl's School in the parish of St. James, every student stood at the ready to join in the celebration of Queen Elizabeth II's coronation. Our uniforms were clean and pressed, every pleat creased in sameness. A band of navy and white moved in unison. Especially on this occasion, not that we dared behave otherwise, order was maintained; decorum the word for the day.

We had prepared for weeks for this moment and now the day had come. Hair and faces shinning, shoes polished, we were lined up by form. Even the carefully manicured grounds and plump blooming flowers seemed to wait in eagerness to please. A short distance down the street, at Saint Silas Boy's School, rows of khaki-clad young men were under similar command.   Parents, other family and friends, lined the narrow streets to join in homage to the monarchy. Pomp and circumstance filled our hearts with pride...just as our island culture encouraged.

I was quietly jubilant as I waited with my classmates to see the face of our queen's sister, the substitute royal representative for the newly crowned queen. In my naiveté I wondered, would the royal carriage stop? Would she get out so that we could get a good look at her? We curtsied, when before our astonished eyes, instead of a golden coach in glittering splendor I had imagined, a large black car slowly passed, giving us a shadowy glimpse of the tiaraed sovereignty. A slight wave of a gloved hand and in minutes it was over. In a fleeting moment, her Royal Highness, Princess Margaret had passed by our school, continuing on her scheduled route that would eventually take her to other stops on the island and throughout the Caribbean.

Disappointment replaced the butterflies in my stomach as I joined my classmates in our return to the classroom. I understood the best image I would ever get of the monarchy, would be the Queen's likeness on the few coins jingling in my pocket.

Sundays with Mrs. Brayton

If I saw her today, I doubt that I would recognize her. That seems odd to me when I think of the many Sunday hours I spent at her home. What I do know and remember is that she loved to cook.

Mrs. Brayton lived along the way between our house in the Spring and the Pentecostal Church we attended at the Endeavor in Orange Hill. Our family joined that church after Ma decided she no longer wanted to attend the Anglican church in Waterhall. For as long as I remember we had attended Saint James Episcopal Church. It's where I was confirmed. Even though I didn't understand all the pomp and rituals, nor did I like the incense, I did enjoy the music and the colors representing the different seasons of the church. I don't know what made Ma leave St. James. I know I was not happy with the move, especially since St. James was a much shorter walk on Sunday mornings. In addition, the one-hour mass was just long enough, that just when I began to get bored, service was over.

To my surprise, the new church was fun. It was different. The services were lively and noisy…nothing like the solemn masses at St. James. They included revival meetings, where the music and singing urged the congregation to stomp their feet, clap their hands, and rejoice. I grew to love revival meetings; watching people get the power, jumping up and down like they were possessed. And actually, that was the whole idea—to be possessed by the Holy Ghost. Pretty soon we children decided it was time to get into the act. As usual, I was chief among the actors. It's a wonder I didn't break something the way I rocked and shock my three-foot, sixty-something pounds.

There was one downside to good times at Endeavor. The meetings were very long, lasting two or more hours, and we had three of them every Sunday: morning worship, afternoon Sunday school and the nighttime revival.

Well, it was those long hours and the break in between meetings that brought us to Mrs. Brayton every Sunday instead going back to our small village. The Spring, tucked away in the western end of the island of Barbados, was as beautiful as it was isolated. The only mode of transportation was horse and cart and we didn't own one of those. Walking the miles back home and returning in time for afternoon Sunday school was impossible, so we spent the intervening hours at Mrs. Brayton. She wasn't a relative, just a good and generous friend who enjoyed company and loved to cook. She did not hesitate for one moment, to invite us to her home, especially when she considered the distance we had to travel to church every week.

"It's just me and Sheila, and I always make more than I need for two people, so come nuh." Her smile widened, exposing one perfectly even gold tooth among her otherwise white teeth.

We soon fell into a fixed routine, arriving at Mrs. Brayton's home a short while after she did. As jovial and friendly as she was, she stopped just long enough after meeting to give a quick greeting to everyone she called friend. But since we lived so far away, we had to make time for God, friend and foe on Sunday. So my family was more inclined to linger among friends.

Walking up the steps to Mrs. Brayton's front door, we were met by the pungent aroma of the meal she had started earlier in the day. We were always in awe at how she managed to get things done so easily. But Mrs. Brayton simply said the food just taste better the longer it soaked up its own juice. So she simply picked up where she left off in the morning before starting out to church.

We enjoyed an abundance of different meals with Mrs. Brayton: chicken in a billion different flavorings, roast pork so juicy, I was often tempted to put down my knife and fork and scoop it up with my fingers. There was succulent lamb and boiled potatoes, our island delicacy of fried flying fish with stewed breadfruit and a special treat of frizzed salt fish. But my personal favorite menu was peas and rice seasoned with salted pigtails, fried corned beef with onions and a side dish of slices of red skin, sweet-like-cake white potatoes. Overstuffed from the heavy meal, washed down with a glass of mauby, ginger beer or Ju-C, we relaxed in Mrs. Brayton's front room until time for Sunday school.

The flavor of those meals still lurks somewhere in the recessed memory of my taste buds, never to be duplicated no matter how many times I've tried. I would pay a king's ransom, and cholesterol be dammed, if I could take a step back in time and have one more Sunday afternoon with Mrs. Brayton.

Sing a song of sixpence,
A pocket full of rye;
Four-and-twenty blackbirds
Baked in a pie.
When the pie was opened
The birds began to sing.
Was not that a dainty dish
To set before the king?
The king was in his counting-house,
Counting out his money;
The queen was in the parlour,
Eating bread and honey.
The maid was in the garden,
Hanging out the clothes;
'Long came a blackbird
And snapt off her nose.

The Monkey Jar and Me

I'm not sure how the job of filling the monkey jar became mine, but each day that's just what I was required to do. I was small for my age, but at some point, I must have looked as though I was capable of handling this responsibility. In the evening just around dusk I walked about a half-mile to the standpipe; or as we locals called it: "the pipe." There I filled my pail with the clean fresh spring water and carried it back to the house on my head that was protected with an expertly rolled head pad. The pad was so cleverly rolled that the pail would sit securely on my head even without my having to hold it. It was a "Look Ma, no hands," act as I strolled back to the house.

The monkey jar was an important fixture in any island home. Without refrigeration to keep things cold, this was the only way to enjoy a thirst-quenching drink of cold water at any time, but especially late at night. So important was monkey jar, it occupied a special shelf inside the house and used for no other purpose. To this day I don't know how it got its name or why we shortened it to just, "the monkey," because, clearly it bore no resemblance to its four-legged, long-tailed namesake.

One evening after returning from my trip to the pipe, I decided to show off my balancing act to my cousin. Being the devil he was, he waited until I put the pail down and tipped it over on its side, emptying it of every drop of water. I complained to Ma, but all she said was, "Ya better get back to de pipe 'fore night come."

My second trip to the pipe lost its charm. By then my friends and walking mates had completed their job and had long returned home. Here I was alone at the standpipe, surrounded on all sides by trees, sugar cane and a gully. Darkness was creeping in and I was scared to the core. I made that second trip in record time. I held a tight grip to the pail on my head, but moved so fast, I lost almost half of the water on the way back home; it was not nearly as neat as my first run.

This chore was usually fun for me: there was always something to divert my attention from the job itself. Along the way to the pipe I might pause to admire Miss Zaleeka's beautiful flower garden or maybe I was tempted to pick a mango from the Brathwaite's mango tree. Or I might spend the time talking with my friend Gerty about nothing in particular. But this night on that second trip, none of that was taking place. This time around, there was none of the swaggering "no hands" for me. Making it home in record time, I completed the job of filling the jar. On the soffit above my kitchen cabinet sits a small monkey jar that I purchased a few years back while visiting my island home. I look lovingly at it every now and then and there's a smile on my face as I recall those trips to the pipe. Now, even the smallest chattel house in Barbados comes equipped with an inside water tap and heaven forbid—bottled water. Ah, technology...not nearly as exotic!

Uncle Beresford and the Ghost

Uncle Beresford was an undertaker. He didn't look the part though. He was a big man: plump with a jolly round face and a devilish smile when he chose to favor us with one. I can't remember him in anything else but his black suit with a pocket watch hanging from his weskit. I was in awe of this giant of a man—great Uncle on my mother's side. My behavior was extra respectful whenever I was in his presence. My long-awaited immigration to America presented the opportunity to do just that: I would be spending a few days at his house.

The house was perfectly situated for easy travel to and from Bridgetown, the capital. Also having the use of Uncle's large black car made the repeated visits to the government offices, doctors and other vital officials more convenient than it would have been from my country home, miles away. Because we had no car, a trip to Bridgetown meant an all-day affair---half of which was walking to and from the bus that would take us there. Aside from the joy of planning for my trip, I was thrilled with the special attention and the time to be on my own, sort of. On this occasion, Ma, my guardian, did not accompany me. She deemed it more logical to remain at home to attend to other responsibilities. Another bonus to this stay at Uncle was the chance to spend some time in such close proximity to his dry goods store and rum shop, just next door to the house; only a walkway separated the buildings. I had my fill of sugar cakes and Ju-C, the favorite island drink, second only to rum, and I soaked up a world so unlike the one I was accustomed to. There was a constant flow of people in and out of the store; the still, cricket-filled evenings of country living were replaced with the mutterings of the inebriated and the click-clack of domino tiles. It was a special time, never to be forgotten, and all was going well until one night.

I was sound asleep when I was awakened by the disquieting sense that someone or something was lurking next to my side of the bed. I opened my eyes, and aided by the slits of moonlight through the jalousie, I got a hazy vision of a fair skinned woman with light-colored hair looking down at me. She wasn't threatening; she seemed to be studying me. I stifled the urge to scream as I scrambled to get up and called to Uncle.

His gravelly response, "it was nothing, you must have been dreaming" did little to reassure me, but I accepted his explanation and went back to bed. By now, of course, the lady was gone. Early the following morning I was standing on the veranda watching the people waiting on queue for the bus that would take them to Bridgetown. I stared in surprise at one woman among them. One minute she was there and then she was gone. I didn't see her get on the bus. Could it be? No, now I must really be imagining things, I reasoned, and I never said anything to Uncle. What could I say?

And so I thought I had grown accustomed to my surroundings: finding things of his trade in this drawer or that corner. Also after my experience with the lady of the night, nothing else could frighten me, right? Wrong! One morning I took it upon myself to empty the chamber pot that we used during the night. I didn't ask any questions. I just picked it up and headed to the back of the yard to dispose of the contents in the outdoor toilet. Uncle's property was pretty large and so there were a number of doors and gates inside the paling. With chamber pot in hand, I opened the first door I came to and to my surprise, found no exit to the toilet. Instead, there in front of me were two coffins neatly arranged in the dark shed-like structure. I don't know about now, but back then folks in Barbados were unreasonably afraid of the dead, which was also known as the duppy. I was no exception. I dropped that chamber pot and just about flew back to the house as fast as my two skinny legs could carry me. I was not ready for what I might have found in the coffins. I didn't mention that to Uncle either.

There came a time after I'd been in America a while, when I was questioned about my last days on the island. Of course my ghost experience was the lead story in my recital. My mother's response was logical. She said it probably was one of Uncle's special friends. She went on to surmise that the woman no doubt heard that someone was staying at the house and not knowing it was a young child, decided to come and see for herself. I asked why Uncle would not have told her about me, and more important, why would she wait till the dead of night (pardon the pun) to investigate, but my mother answered that too. She said it was normal for the men not to explain their actions and didn't feel it necessary to tell her who I was. But like Uncle's conclusion that I was dreaming, I wasn't satisfied with my mother's explanation either. I was convinced that my visitor may have been at Uncle's home before that night, but not as a living guest.

Lavender's blue,
Diddle diddle,
Lavender's green,
When I am king,
Diddle diddle,
You shall be queen.

Lavender's green,
Diddle diddle,
Lavender's blue,
If you love me,
Diddle diddle
I will love you

Leaving

February 11, 1958---The day is finally here. I'm awake but I keep my eyes closed from the darkness. From the next room I hear Da's grating snores amidst the soft noises of the long night. I try not to move so I won't wake my sleeping bedmates, Jennie and Esmee. As I lay quietly in the dark, I think. At the end of the day, I will be in America.

My dream is coming true. No more will I sit in the field with the grazing sheep, and my imaginings of what America will be like. Never again will my classmates tease me for claiming someone else's mother as my own and no longer will I have to steal away to the front room to look at the gray picture sitting on Ma's lace covered table. Under glass in a silver trimmed frame, my mother wears a dress that twirls around her legs and a furry cape around her shoulder. Her hat, perched to the side, has a veil that falls just at the edge of her eyebrows, and she has a smile so pretty it makes me hug myself, as though it was meant just for me. I have stared at that picture many times with a deep longing in my heart. I imagine mother's arms holding me as close as she is holding the cape around her shoulders. I hug myself as my daydreams mix with my memories. My best memory is getting the box from America at Christmas. Our island customs do not include exchanging gifts, so the delivery became an awaited ritual. It meant that it was December and just like the tropical rains that would surely fall, the postman would deliver "the box." Digging deep inside, I would pull out the familiar container of candy; its scent so pungent that I could smell it long before I touched it. Then one Christmas, nestled among the paper was the doll. She looked just like the pictures in the storybooks – and nothing like anyone I ever saw in person with her golden hair and sparkly blue eyes. My joy didn't last. Ma put her away, *to keep her safe*, and all I could do from that day on was look and wish.

In America, I'll have all the candy I want and maybe a new doll. That's what I think as my anxiety builds and I try not to move. When was morning going to get here?

I try to imagine more of what America is like, but instead my mind goes back to two days earlier when Ma decided to surprise me with a special meal. She was going to make stewed chicken. I love chicken. I would chew on the bones until there was nothing left but fine chips.

"When are you going to tro'way dat bone? There is nuffin left on it." I didn't care what anyone said, I didn't stop sucking on the bones 'till I was satisfied I had gotten all the meat and flavor from them.

That day I had a strange feeling about the chicken I was about to eat, because I soon realized my pet chicken was not running around the yard as usual. Whenever I was in the yard, she could be found nearby looking for some treat from me. I got up and went searching. I looked under the cellar, behind the pig pen and the coops. Nothing. No chicken. I called...here chick chick, here chick chick, and still nothing.

"Ma, where is my chicken?"

"In de pot."

That was the end of my dinner that night. Even when the family tried to impress upon me that I couldn't take the chicken to America, I could not be comforted.

****

I now force myself to keep my emotions quiet. I do not want to start crying all over again. Suppose they tell me I can't go to America. Then what would I do? I'd never get to see my mother. I need to think about something else, so I think instead about my trip to Bridgetown a week earlier.

It was the first time I was allowed to go there by myself. I was so scared. I had never gone anywhere alone before---not even to school. I always had my cousins and friends to walk with. I had gotten up early and instead of dressing in my school uniform as I would on a normal day; I put on my Sunday dress and shoes. I walked the familiar roads to get to the bus, not realizing that when walking alone, the long quiet roads were frightening. Sugarcane fields grew thick and tall on both sides. The stories of The Outman whirled around in my head, but I kept walking, determined to show my new grownup self.

Finally, I reached Waterhall Plantation, the busiest sugarcane factory on the island. It's where I would catch the bus. It is also the place where my cousins and I and our school friends pilfered mangoes from the barb-wired grounds. But I was not interested in mangoes that day. My mission was to get to Bridgetown and do some shopping. Thanks to Sister Gray I had lots of coins in my pockets. She had encouraged everyone in the congregation at church to contribute to a going away gift for me. And since the money would not be useful in America, I had to spend it all. So here I was headed toward noisy Bridgetown where I planned to buy something new to take to America.

I boarded the yellow bus to Bridgetown. Sitting in a window seat, I wanted to make sure I didn't miss anything interesting or unusual as the bus wound its way through the skimpy streets of Orange Hill and through to Westmorland and all the way pass Lancaster gully. Except, this gully, a deep, dark abyss was one place I did not want to view as the bus bounced its way along. The stories of things and people falling in were enough to keep my curiosity in check and my eyes closed as the bus drove pass. After more than an hour's ride, the bus reached the Lower Green, the large parking lot where buses from all parts of the island dropped off their passengers---the last stop. It was also the place I would return to get the bus to go back home.

My earlier confidence deserted me when I reached Bridgetown. I had no idea how to maneuver the crowded crisscrossing streets. I took no chances in getting lost. From the bus stand, I walked up the same side of the street from which I had left the bus. I timidly went into the first big clothing store I came to. I proudly took money from my knotted kerchief and purchased a pair of shoes in my favorite color--blue. I also bought a pocketbook, the first of my very own. With my two purchases I headed back to the bus stand where I planned to get on the first bus back towards Waterhall. Before I could climb on board, I was waylaid by a hawker selling fresh fish. With the last of the money now tucked in my new pocketbook, I purchased all the flying fish it allowed and boarded my bus. It had taken me just about thirty minutes to shop. The trip to and from Bridgetown had taken more than three hours and I had done it all by myself. I was extra proud that I fed the whole family with a big and delicious meal of fried fish and breadfruit that evening.

****

My gratifying but unseen smile broadens to a wide gape as just then the old rooster lets out a cockle doo doo. That's it, morning is here. It's time to get ready to leave for America. Ma makes breakfast, but I'm too excited to eat my two eggs today. Ma convinces me that I need to put something on my stomach because "no telling when you gine eat again this day." I'm dressed. My blue flowered dress with its wide lace-trimmed collar feels soft and silky. My blue patent shoes are a perfect match to my blue beret. I had wanted a blue pocketbook, but settled for the brown one I purchased.

I think it's getting late. Jennie and Esmee left for school long ago, and Da is at work. At last, Uncle Beresford arrives in his big black car. He is an undertaker and he's dressed as he would for a funeral—in black from head to toe, with his pocket watch hanging from his vest. I don't know him to look any other way. As usual, he does not smile. Uncle has had a very important role in my going to America. I stayed at his house in the city when I had to go back and forth for my travel papers.

Staying at Uncle was a so different from my life in the country. The back of his house was the funeral business, but shiny coffin objects could be found just about anywhere in the house. I tried to ignore these things and enjoy what was going on next door instead. From my seat on the veranda, I watched as an assortment of customers went in and out of his other business---the busy rum shop. In the evenings, the familiar sounds of chirping crickets and croaking frogs were replaced by the click-clack of dominoes being slammed on the table by sweaty rummies. And somewhere nearby, the sounds of a tinny steelpan could often be heard. I was anxious to get my passport, but I hated to see my visit to Uncle come to an end. Uncle is all business this morning as he ushers Ma and me into the car. My little suitcase is nestled in the back. There's not much in it—some panties, a nightgown, and a new dress my cousin made just for the occasion.

****

Through the small window in the back of the car I take a long last look at my chattel home, fixing all my special places in my memory. Happy as I am to get going, I do not want to forget these things. Something is telling me I may never see them again. The cane flowers are swaying in the breeze and the car seems to glide along the rocky road. Why does it all seem so strange today? It's as if I'm seeing things through a cloud. And I realize there is a cloud---my tears.

The car passes Waterhall and takes the Long Road past the Lodge and through Baywoods village. We drive past the gap where my piano teacher lives. We pass our dear friend Mrs. Brayton, who fed us every Sunday between church service in the morning and Sunday school in the afternoon. I said goodbye to Mrs. Brayton and the whole church on Sunday. There is no one at the church today, but a few people are on the street waving. They know it's me in the big black car. I pass my school and the yard is empty.

School is in session. I wonder what Jennie, Esmee and my friends are doing right now. It's too early for milk and biscuits. They are probably lined up for homework review. I hope they escape the lash today. But maybe they are singing rounds; my favorite is London's Burning. I hope they sing rounds in America.

I can't say goodbye to Ma. She's looks sad. She's been my "mother" since I was two years old when my real mother left for America. Ma is really my great-aunt because she's married to Da, my uncle, whose only farewell words were, "So you're leaving?"

I don't know what to call what I feel for Ma. No one talks about feelings, nothing is explained. Today Ma is stingy with her words, just like Da. And I don't know the words to tell her how I feel; how I understand that for eleven years, she cared for me just as she cared for her own children. I shared equally in everything with Jennie and Esmee, including household tasks and lashes. The one exception Ma made was in making a special meal for me when she made cou-cou. I'm going to miss Ma. I have a funny feeling in my stomach. We don't hug. That's not our way.

"Be good," Ma says through her tears. "Don't forget your manners and don't forget me."

****

I'm finally on the plane. I'm excited. I'm afraid. Everyone around me is very kind. They reassure me that everything is going to be okay. For the long hours I'm in the air I'm comforted by any adult within whispering distance from me and I begin to feel okay. I look out at the clouds and sometimes I look down to see the brown outline of islands below or the ripples of the blue ocean. I'm too excited to sleep.

I arrive at Idlewild in New York. It is dark and the lights outside the window are like Stars on a moonlit night back home. I see other passengers wearing coats as they walk out of the plane. I'm wearing my pretty blue dress with my blue ankle socks and blue patent shoes. The stewardess looks at me with a strange look and as she pulls out a blanket and drapes it over me, she says, "This will keep you warm."

I drag the blanket behind me as I follow the crowd out of the plane. Cold air whips about me and I shiver as I walk in the open air between the plane and the door to Customs and the baggage area. I wait a long time for my suitcase. Finally, it arrives. It's the last one on the carousel. I look around. There is no one here to get me. What should I do? I look up to see some people waving at me. Where do I go? How do I get to them? Then I hear someone tell me to walk through the glass door. I see no handle. How do I open it I wonder?

"Just keep walking," the voice says to my unspoken question. And so I do. The doors part as if by magic. Just outside the glass door I see her---the picture in the silver frame---my mother! She rushes towards me and when we meet she wraps me in a not long enough hug and a long fluffy coat. I feel strange, warm and happy—and I wonder if Ma knows I'm in America.

What is it?

- **Cou-cou** – A meal made of finely ground corn.
- **Dat** – That
- **De** – The
- **Fatpork** – Soft purple pulpy fruit. It is similar in texture to a ripe peach and also has a hard pit
- **Gooseberry** – A yellow hard pitted, fruit with sections. It could be compared to a cherry, except it is very tart
- **Lorry** – common term for a truck
- **Poor-great** – Financially poor, but carrying oneself in a haughty manner
- **Saltfish** – Salted, dried cod
- **Soursop** – A green fruit with a hard, knotty outer shell. The inside is soft and milky. The texture could be compared to a very ripe mango
- **Sweet,** or often, **Too Sweet** – This expression means something is beyond wonderful
- **This, That and De Third** – Sometimes, **Dis, Dat and De Tird** means there are too many things to list separately
- **Turn cornmeal** – to stir or mix meal until smooth
- **Wuhlass** – An exclamation of wonder or surprise; same as saying, 'Oh my!'
- **Washboard** – A wooden grooved board used in place of a washing machine. An item of clothing was rubbed back and forth on the board in order to release any soil
- **Wuddah** – Would have

Old King Cole was a merry old soul
And a merry old soul was he
He called for his pipe
And he called for his bowl
And he called for his fiddlers three
Every fiddler, he had a fiddle
And a very fine fiddle had he
Oh, there's none so rare
As can compare
With King Cole and his fiddlers three

The Monkey Jar

The unglazed earthenware jar is a traditional Barbadian water vessel. The origin of the name is unknown but it is found in many Caribbean countries. The pot is thought to have originated in Africa. Homes without running water or refrigeration, used this jar to store water for drinking.

'Monkey, as it is commonly known, is made from local terra cotta clay and fired to approximately 2000°F. Because the clay is slightly porous, it allows some of the water to penetrate the body-thus making the exterior cold. This causes the water on the inside to become cold and remain so for several hours.

Thirty days hath September
April June and November
All the rest has thirty-one
Except February alone
Which has twenty-eight days clear
And twenty-nine in each leap year

A reasonable facsimile of the chattle house I called home. It even comes with three small children who could easily be my cousins and me.

I had a little nut tree,
Nothing would it bear,
But a silver nutmeg,
And a golden pear.

The King of Spain's daughter
Came to visit me,
And all for the sake
Of my little nut tree.

I skipped over water,
I danced over sea,
And all the birds in the air,
Couldn't catch me.

Barbados – 21 miles long and a smile wide
Capital City– Bridgetown, St. Michael

Sleep, my child and peace attend thee,
All through the night.
Guardian angels God has sent thee,
All through the night.
Soft the drowsy hours creeping,
Hill and dale in slumber sleeping,
I, my loving vigil keeping,
All through the night.

While the moon her watch is keeping
All through the night
While the weary world is sleeping
All through the night
O'er thy spirit gently stealing
Visions of delight revealing
Breathes a pure and holy feeling
All through the night

Made in United States
Troutdale, OR
06/12/2024

20500214R00037